HEART
OF HOPE
A DIRECTED JOURNAL

by JoAnn Streeter Shade

OTHERS
PRESS

Heartwork of Hope: A Directed Journal

Library of Congress Control Number: 2006902485

ISBN 089216106X, 1-59971-734-4

Printed in the United States of America

Heartwork of Hope is a wonderful resource for spiritual growth and renewal. The author's integrative use of Scripture, excerpts from literature and references to film and music provides a holistic approach. Whether used for individual or group spiritual formation, this directed journal opens new possibilities for the soul to breathe the presence of God.

Elaine A. Heath, Ph.D.
McCreless Assistant Professor of Evangelism
Perkins School of Theology
Southern Methodist University

Heartwork of Hope is a treasure of a tool for discovering the "more" that God has for you in His kingdom story. I have long felt the importance of encouraging believers to remember God's faithfulness and reflect on how He continues to guide each of us into new avenues of service and spiritual truth. For those who don't know where to begin, pick up a copy of *Heartwork of Hope*. In each chapter, the reader is guided through exercises that require soul searching and are reinforced by Scripture and excellent quotations. But beware! You can't just sit back and read this book, it must be digested and experienced. And don't be surprised if the result is a transformed life—yours!

Lucinda Secrest McDowell
Speaker and Author
Spa for the Soul—Rejuvenate Your Inner Life

Heartwork of Hope is a great resource for anyone with the courage to look into the depths of their own heart. JoAnn Shade has written a work to help a searching soul ask the right questions that will lead them through their "stuff" and into the heart of God. My clients have greatly benefited from this wonderful work.

Michael Misja, Ph.D.
Psychologist, Clinical Director
North Coast Family Foundation

Heartwork of Hope is both a treasure to mine and a trail to follow. Walking through its pages opens up the truth in personal experience. At the same time it discloses the riches others have to offer. JoAnn Shade sprinkles the book with wisdom garnered from storehouses old and new—her own musing, honored authors, pop music, and recent films. Follow the gleam that is here and watch your hopes come to life.

Jerry R. Flora, Th.D.
Professor Emeritus of Theology and Spiritual Formation
Ashland Theological Seminary

The words in this journal flow from my own journey toward hope. Its seeds were planted in a counselor training course taught by Dr. Michael Misja, and fleshed out through interaction with the North Coast Family Foundation staff and classmates, as well as with my seminary ally Dena Schnupp. Others have walked alongside me for parts of the journey, providing strength, comfort, and discomfort as needed. Through it all, the continued support of my husband and sons is an essential part of my walk. Thank you, dear ones.

With joy,

Major JoAnn Shade, M.A.

AN INVITATION TO
HEARTWORK

Consider yourself invited! This directed journal is designed to invite you to do the "heartwork" of hope in light of your personal pilgrimage. The heartwork (reading, writing, thinking, feeling, praying) begins with an exploration of the journey—where you've been and where you long to go. It will give you the opportunity to look at your own heart in connection with the presence of God in your life, as well as in the way you see yourself. It will help you consider how you have sought purpose, how you wrestle with the desires for integrity and justice, and how you interact in relationships with the people in your life. It concludes with a focus on hope, for it is hope that gives the people of God the ability to faithfully seek and follow Him.

Each section of the journal provides space to respond to questions that will begin the process of reflection, introspection, and vision development for you. Answer those that speak to you, and then use those answers as stepping stones for further thought, conversation, and prayer. Write honestly, spontaneously, and deeply. Space has been provided at the end of each section for your heartwork—thinking, writing, feeling, praying.

> I have seen many different kinds of people make the discovery that their original questions were only tickets to enter the theater. Once inside, the tickets were no longer necessary or interesting.
>
> *Thomas Moore*

Each topic is considered in the following progression:

The Prelude introduces the subject in each section. You will get a chance to explore the journey and to consider the way you see your self-image and the essence of God. You also will be able to contemplate the roles of purpose, integrity, and relationship, and how they work together to create a hope-filled life.

The Reflecting Pool provides the opportunity to reflect on the past, to consider the impact people and events have had upon your journey.

The Introspective Corner is the place for examination of current, here-and-now issues, not as a self-absorbed, navel-gazing project, but as a healthy inventory of where you are.

> I get glimpses of myself in other people's eyes.
> I've looked for an image in someone else's mirror,
> and so have avoided seeing myself.
>
> *Madeleine L'Engle*

An Emerging Vision gives the framework for developing a dream or vision that will encourage you to be intentional in choices for the future, in faith.

> We shall not cease from exploration
> And the end of all our exploring
> Will be to arrive where we started
> And know the place for the first time.
>
> *T.S. Elliot*

To Join the Dance provides direction in selecting actions that follow from the reflection, examination, and vision development, because knowing which direction we want to take doesn't necessarily get us any farther along the path or move us any closer to our destination. When the band strikes up a polka at a wedding, we can stay in our seats, tapping our feet, or we can get up and dance!

One of my fond memories of pre-school days was a daily visit to Romper Room on channel 7. I loved Miss Molly, and would do whatever she said. My favorite part was when she would say, "Mr. Music, please ..." and the music would begin. The children on the TV set would begin to move with the music, not in a sophisticated dance, but rather with a joyous movement of body that came from within—and I would join them!

The journey progresses when we accept the invitation to move onto the dance floor. Each section of this journal will have **First Steps,** ideas that can be used to give "feet" to our hearts and minds, that can help us find ways to listen for the music and to enter the dance.

> How beautiful on the mountains are the feet of those who bring good news, who proclaim peace, who bring good tidings, who proclaim salvation, who say to Zion, "Your God reigns!"
>
> *Isaiah 52:7*, NIV

> Who knows in what inspired way the heart, mind, spirit of the herald came to receive the good tidings of peace and salvation in the first place, but as to the question whether he would actually do something about them—put his money where his mouth was, his shoe leather where his inspiration was—his feet were the ones that finally had to decide. Maybe it is always so.
>
> *Frederick Buechner*

Bread for the Soul will offer Scripture, books, films, and music to provide additional nourishment. Choose what intrigues you. Follow the thread these resources give you.

> Lord, I hunger for your holiness,
> To be fashioned in my heart today,
> Purify my thoughts and motives,
> Mold me in your hands, as clay.
> Feed me with the bread of heaven,
> Fresh from the hearthstone of your heart,
> Sustain my body
> Renew my soul,
> Feed me 'til I want no more.
>
> *jas**

* Throughout the journal JoAnn Shade's own poems are signed "jas."

Pause for a moment and consider what it is you are hungry for. Write out two or three ways in which you hunger for God to meet you as you turn the pages of this journal.

Example: I am hungry to find a passion for ministry in a specific way. I long to see God in a new way.

_____

_____

_____

_____

_____

_____

_____

_____

_____

_____

A wise woman who was traveling in the mountains found a precious stone in a stream. The next day she met another traveler who was hungry, and the wise woman opened her bag to share her food. The hungry traveler saw the precious stone and asked the woman to give it to him. She did so without hesitation. The traveler left, rejoicing in his good fortune. He knew the stone was worth enough to give him security for a lifetime. But, a few days later, he came back to return the stone to the wise woman. "I've been thinking," he said. "I know how valuable this stone is, but I give it back in the hope that you can give me something even more precious. Give me what you have within you that enabled you to give me this stone."

Unknown

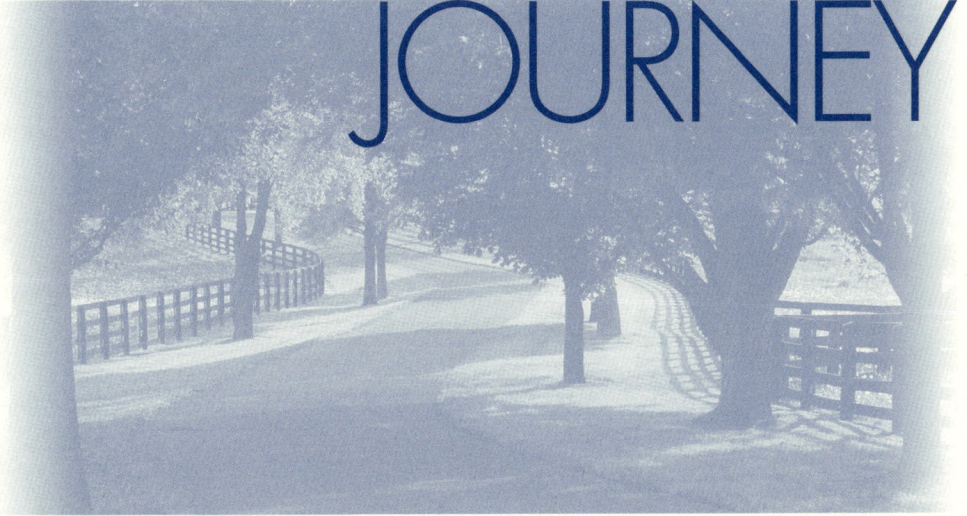

JOURNEY

THE PRELUDE

What is life about? Is it a series of disjointed events with no purpose, "absolutely pointless," as the spokesman in Ecclesiastes proposes?

Is life only a shadow, "signifying nothing," as Macbeth claims?

Out, out, brief candle.
Life's but a walking shadow;
a player that struts and frets his hour upon the stage
and then is heard no more: it is a tale
told by an idiot, full of sound and fury,
signifying nothing.

William Shakespeare

Or is life a connected journey that can be made with intention and integrity?

It will take courage, strength, trust, and discipline to travel successfully; in other words, it is in the journey that spiritual character is forged.

Luther Smith

I have to believe that life is a purposeful journey that has a place in the grand drama that is the Kingdom of God. It continues to amaze me as to how economical God has been in my journey. He hasn't wasted anything! In the midst of the going, I sometimes think that He has no clue as to where He is taking me (funny how I think that because I'm confused, God must be as well). However, I've found that if I can muster up the courage to hang on, if only by my fingernails, the day will come when I can recognize the pattern of His grace. And oh, what a tapestry!

Trust in the Lord with all your heart,
and do not rely on your own insight.
In all your ways acknowledge him,
and he will make straight your paths.

Proverbs 3:5-6, NRSV

The new country is where you are called to go, and the only
way to go there is naked and vulnerable. It seems that you keep
crossing and recrossing the border... Risk a few more steps into
the new country, trusting that each time you enter it, you will
feel more comfortable and be able to stay longer.

Henri Nouwen

My children used to love singing along with the "Wee Sing" tapes when we traveled
in the car. One of their favorites was "She waded in the water," a song that told the
story of a little girl who waded in the water and got her toes all wet, her ankles wet,
her knees wet, and with the final line of the song "she finally got her bathing suit
wet—yet!" I find myself like that little girl at times, hesitant to enter new things, to
get my bathing suit wet. But as God has continued to breathe His Spirit into my life
on a daily basis, I've realized that sometimes the whisper comes, "Put your toe in
the water today," while other times, His voice is loud and clear—"Get the bathing
suit wet—JUMP!" I pray that when the Spirit says "plunge in," my response will
be obedient, to dive quickly and deeply.

Ezekiel 47:1-6 tells of stepping into the water—ankle-deep, knee-deep, waist
deep, and ultimately, over the head. Jesus says, "come to the water…"

Are you ready? Write about your reaction to the invitation to plunge in.

_____

_____

_____

_____

_____

_____

THE REFLECTING POOL

Where have I been?

They sought a way to God that was uncharted and freely chosen, whom they alone could find.

Thomas Merton

Your journey in life has brought you to this day. Reflect on some of the influences that have had an impact on you.

Which learning experiences stand out for you?

_____

_____

_____

_____

_____

_____

_____

_____

What activities (hobbies, sports, etc.) have brought you the most pleasure?

_____

_____

_____

_____

_____

_____

_____

_____

In remembering the homes you have lived in, where were the places of warmth for you?

_____

_____

_____

_____

_____

_____

How have your vocational choices shaped you as a person?

_____

_____

_____

_____

_____

_____

Which of these images best reflects your journey?

- ☐ a roller coaster
- ☐ the little engine that could
- ☐ bumper-to-bumper traffic
- ☐ a leisurely ride in the country
- ☐ power walking
- ☐ the Boston marathon
- ☐ a hamster's exercise wheel
- ☐ _____

Write about how that felt:

_____

_____

_____

_____

_____

_____

_____

_____

It was a wrong turn at the crossroads,
between the survival of the body and the survival of the soul.
Too many wrong turns and one day you or I might wake up
wondering where we are, how we ever ended up here,
so far from who we once were and once thought we might
become.

Ken Gire

At times, we recognize that we have made poor choices along the way. Write down two choices that may not have been the best decision, explore the impact they have had on your life, and consider how God has worked in you to redeem those choices.

Choice	Impact	How God redeemed it
dropped out of college	could only get dead-end job	gave me the courage to go back to school at age 30

We prefer to read the maps rather than visit the place.
Brennan Manning

In our walk of faith, there are both light and heavy times, times when we feel uplifted and times when we feel overwhelmed. Write or draw about some of these times in your life.

Light	Heavy
birth of my son	serious illness of my father

THE INTROSPECTIVE CORNER

Where am I now?

Today, as I pause by the side of the road, I am:

☐ in a rut, lacking motivation or energy to move in any new direction

☐ on the mountaintop, excited about what today may bring

☐ stuck, up against the wall somewhere in my life

☐ at rest, finding a centered place within

☐ disrupted, feeling undone by something going on in my life

☐ despondent, facing the day with little hope

☐ content, able to put the struggles of life into perspective

As you are at that roadside stop, write about how that feels today.

_____

_____

_____

_____

_____

_____

I want to fly, and I know I can
(deep down inside I do know this)
but I seem to only plod along.
What holds me down?

Joyce Rupp

Just as a hot air balloon is tethered to the ground, we may have ropes that are holding us down. Describe those ropes.

_____

_____

_____

_____

_____

_____

There is an eagle in me that wants to soar,
and there is a hippopotamus in me
that wants to wallow in the mud.

Carl Sandburg

web

how patiently the trap is set
silent, subtle
glistening strands of should and ought
self-propelled expectations weaving their snare of demand
silken threads of syrup-laden voices petrified into chains of iron
gossamer fibers, laced with fear
spin, spider, spin

jas

AN EMERGING VISION

Where am I going?

> How blessed all those in whom you live,
> whose lives become roads you travel;
> They wind through lonesome valleys,
> come upon brooks, discover cool springs
> and pools brimming with rain!
> God-traveled, these roads curve up the mountains
> and at the last turn—Zion!
> God in full view.
>
> *Psalm 84:5-7, The Message*

What is ahead on your journey? While we don't have a crystal ball to see what will be in the future (and it is probably a good thing we don't), we can look to the future with a vision, a hope of where God might possibly take us.

> The great new thing He wanted to do in our lives
> overshadowed whatever our broken starting points were.
>
> *Andrew Comiskey*

Establishing a vision of where I am going must be integrated with the question of who I am becoming (explored more fully in the next section). For now, ask yourself the question: What great new things might God desire for me? Do some brainstorming, on your own or with a friend.

Write down any ideas that come to your heart and mind. There will be time later to sort them out, but for now, let the boundaries go and dream big! Don't let your dreaming be limited by money, education, ability, or lack of courage.

Example: To spend a six-month sabbatical writing a book on a theology of marriage for my denomination

Brainstorm…

Now, choose two dreams from your brainstorming list that give you goose-bumps, or that make you feel most alive, and consider what it would take to get to that destination.

Example:

Dream 1: Apply for sabbatical.

What it would take to get there:
1. Persuade my spouse that I should do it.
2. Arrange for a place to stay for a few weeks alone.
3. Do preparatory study on what others have written.

Dream 1:

What it would take to get there:

Dream 2:

What it would take to get there:

Based on these potential visions for your life, do you feel as though you are on the right road? Why or why not?

_____

_____

_____

_____

_____

_____

_____

_____

_____

How do you know if any of your dreams are right for you? Consider these tests for each vision:

- ☐ Is it consistent with Scripture?
- ☐ Is it consistent with what I know about God?
- ☐ Is it in line with my gifts and abilities?
- ☐ Is it in opposition to the commitments I have made to God, my spouse, and children?
- ☐ Does it feel right? (While this is not always a valid criterion, we do feel a sense of peace or at least the lessening of unrest when the Spirit of God is at work.)

> Sometimes people need to learn pathways into their own hearts to see what lies there. We are so accustomed to external stimulation and direction that we often place authority outside ourselves. It might be easier to live by someone else's rules or dictates, but in the long run, that life has less integrity. It is far harder, and more significant, to find these unique guidelines that God has set within our hearts.
>
> _Kathy Coffey_

What roadblocks do you see in moving toward your dreams?

Roadblock	How it could be overcome

Commit to paper, and to heart, a Scripture promise that you can claim for your dreams.

My Scripture promise is:

Since we are surrounded by so many examples of faith, we must get rid of everything that slows us down, especially sin that distracts us. We must run the race that lies ahead of us and never give up. We must focus on Jesus, the source and goal of our faith. He saw the joy ahead of him, so he endured death on the cross and ignored the disgrace it brought him.

Hebrews 12:1-2, God's Word

Is this a time to consider changing directions? If so, what new direction is God calling you to?

_____

_____

_____

_____

_____

Which paths are no longer an option?

_____

_____

_____

_____

_____

If it takes exile to teach us such wisdom, then I welcome exile. Only exiles are sufficiently torn from their kingdoms to mend and restore the "best things that cannot be talked about," the near occasions of grace that are always inviting us into something more.

Richard Rohn

Is God calling you toward exile? If so, what might that look like?

_____

_____

_____

_____

_____

_____

If knowing answers to life's questions is absolutely necessary to you, then forget the journey. You will never make it, for this is a journey of unknowables, of enigmas, incomprehensible and unanswered questions, most of all things unfair.

Madame Jeanne Guyon

Write out questions or worries you have about the journey.

_____

_____

_____

_____

_____

_____

_____

Pray about those questions, and articulate your willingness to trust them to God.

Lord God, _____

_____

_____

_____

_____

_____

Find a symbolic way to release those questions and worries, such as tying them to a helium balloon, or tossing stones in a lake or ocean.

TO JOIN THE DANCE

There is nothing, indeed, which God will not do for a man who dares to step out upon what seems to be a mist; though as he puts down his foot he finds a rock beneath him.

F.B. Meyer

What does taking a next step into the mist awaken in you?

hope

fear   excitement

courage

a desire to run

anxiety

frustration   joy!

Traveler, there are no roads.
Roads are made by walking.

Spanish proverb

In contemporary culture, life's journey seems more like a trip on the interstate highway than a stroll down a country lane. Using the metaphor of an interstate highway, consider the following:

Is life passing you by as you crawl in the slow lane, or do you seem to be in the fast lane, speeding past what really matters? Do you need to be intentional in a lane change? Name three specific ways you will change lanes this month.

1. _____

2. _____

3. _____

What is your favorite rest area? (beach, park, porch swing?)

_____

When will you plan to visit your own rest area again?

_____

When you come to a life "construction zone," what is your reaction?

_____

What one area of your life is in need of the orange barrels?

_____

Near large cities, interstate highways have commuter lanes, where each car must have two or more occupants during restricted hours. If you could choose one person to be your companion (other than your spouse or Jesus), who would it be and why?

_____

_____

_____

_____

First steps ...

- Bury the shell of unachieved ambition.
- Write out a personal mission statement.
- Clean out closets with a vengeance.
- Begin a college course.
- Start writing that book that's begging to be written.
- Phone the friend you haven't spoken with in a long time.
- Take God at His word.
- Go on a short-term mission trip.
- Go on a silent retreat.
- Repent.
- Draw a picture of a road that awaits you.
- Read the Psalms of exile (42, 43, 107, 126, 137).
- Go for a walk without any specific destination.
  One way to do this in the city is to go to the corner, flip a coin, and go right (heads) or left (tails).

Stand at the crossroads and look;
Ask for the ancient paths,
Ask where the good way is,
And walk in it,
And you will find rest for your souls.

Jeremiah 6:16, NIV

We journey in increments. We measure our journey in feet and miles, land-marks and destinations. In answering the question, "Where am I going?" what are two or three "first steps" you might take next?

_____

_____

_____

_____

As a commitment to join the dance, a step I will take today is:

_____

_____

_____

_____

A step I will pray about for the future is:

_____

_____

_____

_____

_____

Adestes fideles ...
come, all ye faithful,
and all ye who would like to be faithful,
if only you could,
all ye who walk in darkness and hunger for light.
Have faith enough, hope enough,
despair enough, foolishness enough,
at least to draw near to see for yourself.

Frederick Buechner

Prayer ...

Almighty God, God of Abraham and Sarah, God of Moses, Aaron and Miriam, God of Ruth and Naomi, hear the prayer of my pilgrim heart. In the night, may I choose to follow the path You illuminate for me; in the mists, may I move carefully to seek Your face, and in the darkness, may I cling to who I know You to be, and what I have learned in the light, so that when the dawn comes, I will still be found faithful. In the name of Jesus, my companion on the journey.

Amen.

---

dance, then, wherever you may be
I am the Lord of the dance, said He...

Sydney Carter

Heartwork ...

(space to think, write, pray, feel)

_____

_____

_____

_____

_____

_____

_____

_____

_____

_____

_____

_____

_____

_____

BREAD FOR THE SOUL

Scripture

Psalm 1

Exodus

Ruth

Film

The Shawshank Redemption

Music

"When All Is Said and Done," Geoff Moore

"Find Me in the River," Martin Smith

"God Will Make a Way," Don Moen

"Joy in the Journey," Michael Card

"Lord of the Dance," Sydney Carter

The Written Word

Hinds' Feet on High Places, Hannah Hurnard

Windows of the Soul, Ken Gire

Dear Heart, Come Home, Joyce Rupp

Gift from the Sea, Anne Morrow Lindbergh

The Road Less Traveled, M. Scott Peck

May I Have This Dance? Joyce Rupp

Psalms of My Life, Joseph Bayly

Homesick for Eden: About the Journey of a Soul, Gary W. Moon

The Healing Path, Dan Allender

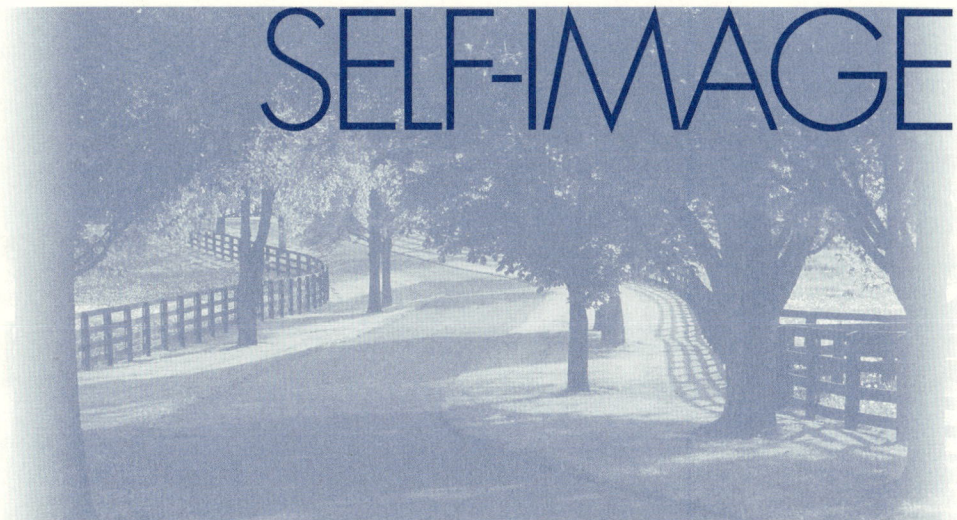

SELF-IMAGE

THE PRELUDE

Who am I?

And we, who with unveiled faces
all reflect the Lord's glory,
are being transformed into his likeness
with ever-increasing glory,
which comes from the Lord, who is the Spirit.

2 Corinthians 3:18, NIV

I know the roles I play, the images I project, and the hats I wear, but who am I really? Am I defined by my roles, my images and my "hats," or is there a center to who I am that is whole, and integrated with the roles, images, and hats? Finding an answer to this question, as fluid as that answer may turn out to be, is essential to our movement towards maturity in Christ.

For a long time, I felt like the juggler in the circus who kept the plates spinning in the air, and each year seemed to bring another plate. They were good plates—my husband, three sons, the desire to write, playing in a musical group, preaching, a demanding ministry, housework, watching the Buffalo Bills, taking classes, composing, reading another book, baking cookies—and then we got a dog! Who was I in the midst of all the plates? Where was my heart for God? Where was my time with God? Where was my feminine soul? It wasn't until I gave myself permission to let the plates fall that I was able to connect with a centeredness within me that remained constant, in spite of outside influences. And it was amazing to realize that sometimes someone else was there to catch one of the plates, and at other times I was able to pick a plate up again after a rest. For some of the plates, I found it truly was time to put them down—or even to let them break!

Jesus came to free you and to create in you a space where you can be with Him. He wants you to live the freedom of the children of God.

Henri Nouwen

THE REFLECTING POOL

Who have I been?

> The Lord said to Jeremiah:
> Before I formed you in the womb I knew you,
> before you were born I set you apart.
>
> *Jeremiah 1:5, NIV*

> Human personality is the reservoir of the most incredible
> feelings and ideas. The message seems to be: ignore it, focus
> on Christ in a way that blots out any deep self-awareness.
> It results in an ostrichlike peace that equips us to relate only to
> fellow pretenders.
>
> *Larry Crabb*

Take time to look through pictures from your childhood and adolescence.
Jot down some words to describe the child you see.

Examples: sassy, kind, scared, chubby, strong

_____

_____

_____

_____

What do you like most about the child you see?

_____

_____

_____

What do you like most about the teenager you see?

_____

_____

_____

Recall happy, playful moments from your childhood. Write them down or draw them. Did you have any nicknames as a child? How did these make you feel?

God does not see us with all the self-imposed limitations we've put on ourselves.

Tim Hansel

God created us as male and female. Often we become confused as to our identity as men and women, swayed by the power of role definitions and cultural expectations. In addition to exploring the question, "Who have I been as a person?" we also are challenged by, "How do I see myself as a man?" or "How do I see myself as a woman?" What do you believe about gender? Are there truly differences?

What messages have you received about being a man or a woman?

Examples: Boys don't cry. A woman needs a man to be happy.

_____

_____

_____

_____

_____

How did—and how do—these messages affect how you see yourself as a man or woman?

Example: I feel really weak if I cry.

_____

_____

_____

_____

_____

Think of a person in your life who seems to be really comfortable with his or her sense of masculinity or femininity. What draws you to that person?

_____

_____

_____

_____

In what situation have you felt uniquely and distinctly feminine or masculine?

_____

_____

_____

_____

_____

_____

In what situation have you felt the most pain as a woman or man?

_____

_____

_____

_____

_____

_____

In what situation have you felt the most joy as a woman or man?

_____

_____

_____

_____

_____

We cannot change men—
we cannot change ourselves—
we can only put ourselves in the presence of
and under the mercy of
the One who can refashion our hearts.

Nancy Groom

THE INTROSPECTIVE CORNER

Who am I?

Let's practice real love …
it's also the way to shut down debilitating self-criticism,
even when there is something to it.
For God is greater than our worried hearts
and knows more about us
than we do ourselves.

1 John 3:18, 20, The Message

Generally speaking, if you want to know who you really are as
distinct from who you like to think you are, keep an eye on
where your feet take you.

Frederick Buechner

One of the paradoxes of our existence is that we are made in the image of
God, but we also have a bent toward sin. We have both dignity and depravity.
At times, we wallow in our sinfulness, and cannot see any light in ourselves.
At other times, we become our own gods, only able to see what is good.

dust and glory,
nothingness and grace,
refiner's gold in earthen vessels

jas

Humans are at the same time worm food and stardust.

Leonard Sweet

Make a list of characteristics in yourself in which you see dignity. Match that with a list of characteristics that show your depravity. Try to keep the lists the same length.

Dignity	Depravity

Consider which list came easier to you. Did you struggle to see the depravity in your life and heart? If so, are you ready to look deeper? Be specific in your praying: "Lord, show me my sin." Be aware that He will faithfully answer that prayer. Write it out:

_____

_____

_____

_____

_____

_____

In your sin, how do you attempt to hide from God?

_____

_____

_____

_____

_____

_____

Another way to see what is within is to ask a trusted friend, or if you're really brave, your spouse or teenager. What might he or she say?

_____

_____

_____

_____

_____

_____

nothing in my hand I bring,
simply to thy cross I cling;
naked, come to thee for dress,
helpless, look to thee for grace,
foul, I to the fountain fly;
wash me, Saviour, or I die

Augustus Montague Toplady

There are many people who can easily see their sin, but struggle to see themselves with dignity—a person formed in the image of God. When we deny our dignity, we fail to accept the truth of Scripture and refuse to acknowledge the redemptive power of God.

> Who are the hardest people to get along with? Those who don't like themselves. Because they don't like themselves, they don't like others, and they're hard to get along with. Low self-esteem wrecks interpersonal relationships more than anything else I know. If you have low self-esteem, you ask another human being to do for you what no other person can do—to make you feel adequate and able—when you are already convinced that you are inadequate and unable.
>
> *David Seamonds*

Did you struggle to see the dignity in your life and heart? If so, are you are ready to look deeper? Be specific in your praying: "Lord, show me Your image reflected in my life." Be ready—God will answer that prayer as well. Write out that prayer.

_____

_____

_____

_____

_____

_____

Perhaps you need to ask a trusted friend or spouse how they see the image of Christ reflected in your life. What would that person say?

_____

_____

_____

_____

_____

_____

who am I? who am I?
the question echoes still,
child of God, image bearer,
called to seek His will.
who I am is named and kept
in His shepherd love,
precious child, beloved one,
in the Father's eyes
beloved, in the Father's eyes
made worthy through Christ's sacrifice
sustained secure in His embrace
abiding in forgiving grace
beloved, in the Father's eyes

jas

My husband and I spent a number of years serving in a pastoral role to a drug and alcohol rehabilitation program. One day, a man testifying to God's work in his life said, "This morning I looked in the mirror, and I didn't have to duck." Some days, I just don't look in the mirror … yet there are other days when I can look in the mirror and smile!

Becoming the beloved means letting the truth of our belovedness become enfleshed in everything we think, say or do. It entails a long and painful process of appropriation, or, better, incarnation. As long as being the beloved is little more than a beautiful thought or lofty idea … nothing really changes. What is required is to become the beloved in the commonplaces of my daily existence, to close the gap that exists between what I know myself to be and the countless specific realities of everyday life. Becoming the beloved expresses the core truth of our existence.

Henri Nouwen

When my children were young, we would go to a mall outside of Philadelphia where there was a merry-go-round. When they were old enough to ride by themselves, I remember that each time they came past where I was standing, I smiled and waved to them. In my wave was the message — Mommy's still here — and I still love you. They were my boys, and I so delighted in their enjoyment of the ride and in being able to know them and to love them, just the way they were. Sounds like God....

God delights in you. What is your reaction to that statement?

_____

_____

_____

_____

_____

_____

He will take great delight in you!

Zephaniah 3:17, NIV

AN EMERGING VISION

Who might I become?

And so, dear brothers and sisters,
I plead with you to give your bodies to God.
Let them be a living and holy sacrifice—
the kind he will accept.
When you think of what he has done for you,
is this too much to ask?
Don't copy the behavior
and customs of this world,
but let God transform you into a new person
by changing the way you think.
Then you will know what God wants you to do,
and you will know how good
and pleasing
and perfect
his will really is.

Romans 12:1-2, NLT

Think about those people you know who are in their "golden" years. List some you would like to be like "when you grow up" and why.

Name	Why I'd like to be like her/him
1.	
2.	
3.	
4.	
5.	

In my work with women who have spent a long time in poverty and on public assistance, it is often very difficult for them to see the gifts and abilities they have. When I ask them to make a list of their gifts and abilities, they freeze, because they can see very little positive in themselves. When I begin to read a list of a couple of hundred gifts and abilities, pointing out what I see in them, they start to respond: "Yeah, I can do that; oh, that's me."

Each one of us has been given gifts, talents, and natural abilities from the Master Creator. We have also developed skills and abilities as we have moved through life. What do you see as your gifts and abilities? Make a list of at least five gifts that you have been graced with, from the practical (makes great chocolate chip cookies) to the less tangible (I can bring comfort to someone who has been hurt by gossip).

1.

2.

3.

4.

5.

Can you now believe in your own giftedness?

As you consider your gifts, abilities, personality, interests, and heritage, write a description of who you desire to become over the next five years. Be specific, not just in accomplishments and achievements, but in character.

I wrote the following list in my journal:

1. *I long to be a godly woman, secure in my faith.*
2. *I will place value upon my self-worth.*
3. *I desire to find healthy ways of dealing with my anger.*
4. *I will treat my children with love and respect.*
5. *I want to share in a healthy, secure, mutually caring relationship with my husband.*
6. *I don't want to be bound by what I perceive to be role expectations within my church.*

Now it's your turn. Finish this sentence: In the next five years, I truly long to become ...

_____

_____

_____

_____

_____

_____

_____

_____

_____

_____

TO JOIN THE DANCE

The song he wanted to sing has never happened—
he spent his days stringing and unstringing his instrument.

Rebindranath Tagore

First steps ...

- Sit quietly with the unnamed stirrings within you.

- Spend 24 hours totally alone.

- Ask God to show you your heart.

- Draw or paint a self-portrait.

- Speak out loud the deepest longings of your heart to God—
  or to another person.

- Ask a close friend to think of what he or she would say at your funeral.

- Explore the Enneagram, an ancient tradition of personal understanding and growth. (See Rohr's book listed in Bread for the Soul.)

- Sing the song you truly want to sing out loud, even if only in the shower!

- Learn about the Myers-Briggs personality inventory, and take the test if you are able.

- Ask your teenager who you are—but only if you're prepared to hear what he or she has to say without wanting to retaliate.

- Explore the creation account in Genesis to discover what it says about self, men and women.

- Form a vision of who you would like to become. Does it have an enthusiasm for life, a passion for God, an openness to truth, and a longing for transformation?

- Ask yourself what your dog or cat could say to describe you if they could talk.

- Consider the fruit of the Spirit in Galatians 5:22-23, and choose one to pursue in depth.

You have to be willing to live your loneliness, your incompleteness, your lack of total incarnation fearlessly, and trust that God will give you the people to keep showing you the truth of who you are.

Henri Nouwen

As a commitment to join the dance, a step I will take today in seeking to know myself more deeply is:

_____

_____

_____

_____

_____

_____

A step I will consider for the future is:

_____

_____

_____

_____

_____

_____

We have this treasure in jars of clay to show that this all-surpassing power is from God and not from us.

2 Corinthians 4:7, NIV

Prayer ...

Precious Lord, take my hand through the journey of self-exploration. Save me from the self-centered bellybutton-gazing that seeks to exalt the temple of self. Keep me from pride and arrogance, in which I deny my depravity. But also keep me from the self-degradation that refuses to recognize the dignity within myself that comes from being created in Your image. Might I ever seek to reflect Your Spirit residing within me. In the name of the One who knows my heart better than I do,

Amen.

Heartwork ...

(space to think, write, pray, feel)

_____

_____

_____

_____

_____

_____

_____

_____

_____

_____

_____

_____

_____

_____

_____

_____

BREAD FOR THE SOUL

Scripture

Mark 10:17-31

Music

"Holy, You Are Still Holy," Kim Hill

"I'm Growing," Wayne Watson

"Rock of Ages," as sung by Glad

The Written Word

"When I Am an Old Woman, I Shall Wear Purple,"
    Sandra Haldeman Martz

Self-Esteem: A Family Affair, Jean Issley Clarke

You Are Special, Max Lucado

Man's Search for Meaning, Victor Frankl

Inside Out, Larry Crabb

The Enneagram, Richard Rohr

GOD ESSENCE

THE PRELUDE

Who is God?

You will seek the Lord your God,
and you will find him if you search after him
with all your heart and soul.

Deuteronomy 4:29, NRSV

The way we see God impacts how we relate to Him and to each other. Consider these images, and the potential results.

Seeing God as a **severe judge,** we might live with a legalistic perspective and an overabundance of fear and guilt.

Seeing God as a **shepherd,** we could be content to be plump sheep or helpless lambs.

Seeing God primarily as **"somewhere out there,"** we might feel that we cannot experience Him in any tangible way.

Seeing God as our **companion,** He could become our "good buddy," and we could lose sight of His glory.

How can we find a way of seeing God that embraces all of His attributes, His presence, and His story?

THE REFLECTING POOL

Who was God to me?

> Jesus called the infants to him and said, "Don't stop the children from coming to me! Children like these are part of the Kingdom of God."
>
> *Luke 18:16, God's Word*

> Because of our physical hunger, we know there is bread. Because of our spiritual hunger, we know there is Christ.
>
> *Malcolm Muggeridge*

My earliest images of God were:

_____

_____

_____

_____

_____

_____

Often, we initially see God as having characteristics of our early caregivers, especially mother and father.

In what ways does God seem to be like your mother?

_____

_____

_____

_____

_____

mother

source of solace for skinned knees, broken hearts
balm of gilead anointing the weary, the wounded
paraclete of everlasting arms
comforter

milk of ample breast awaits the suckling babe
meager bread and fish swelled to nourish faceless crowd
bruised body, spilled blood, poured and partaken still
nurture-giver

fragile chicks nestled beneath almighty wings
embrace of strength upholding those in peril
hedge of grace surrounding the remnant faithful
protector

luminous glow of porchlight on moonless night
lavished love sustained from ocean-depth
carved name on pierced palm
keeper

jas

A happy and playful attachment between mother and baby
prepares the child for similar attachments later in life, especially
to God, who is in some sense of surrogate mother — an all
powerful source of love and reassurance.
Andrew Greeley

In what ways does God seem to be like your father?

_____

_____

_____

_____

_____

_____

father

life-giver
source of conception, birthing forth flesh
genesis tension fertile with mercy
incarnational presence made apparent
creation

prodigal-receiver
redemptively waiting, intensely watching
open arms extending in welcoming embrace
home-coming celebration in extravagance
reconciliation

daddy
safe refuge, sanctuary
fragile child enfolded in protective strength
tenderly cradled in compassionate grace
home

jas

If you went to church as a child, take a few moments to recall Sunday School teachers, singing in the junior choir, the pictures in the stained glass windows, the people you sat with in church. Reflecting on that time:

write a poem … draw a picture … record a story … pen a note to someone

Perhaps your childhood did not include any spiritual guidance or church experience, or it may have brought painful incidents associated with religion. Take some time to feel sorrow over that loss, recognizing that you have lost precious occasions of grace, but that God is a God of healing. Write about what you are feeling just now.

_____

_____

_____

_____

_____

_____

_____

Listen to Paul Stookey's "Hymn," hearing the yearning in his words. Attend to the whisper of that yearning in your own heart.

Sunday morning, very bright,
I read your book by colored light
That came into the pretty window picture.

As you reflect upon the people and circumstances that have molded your faith walk, complete the following prayer.

Thank You, God, for _____,

_____,

_____,

_____,

who played such a large role in my encounters with You.

If these people are still alive, find a way to tell them how much they mattered.

Within the Christian tradition, there are various "coming to God" occasions, such as conversion, baptism, and confirmation. There are also less formal times when we have turned a corner or taken a leap of faith. Pause to recall those significant points in your life. Jot down words that describe the sensory impact, such as sights, sounds, smells, tastes, and textures, as well as the spiritual and emotional feelings you experienced.

_____

_____

_____

_____

_____

_____

_____

As a teenager, I wrestled with issues of faith. I was raised in the Presbyterian tradition, began playing the piano at an evangelistic church, and was active in Young Life. From a very early age, I recognized a longing for God, and responded to that in many ways, but I came to a crossroad at a Young Life weekend. We were challenged to find a solitary place in which to face God. I went into the woods on that snowy Saturday afternoon, determined not to come back to the warmth of the meeting room until I knew that my life was His. Like Jacob, I came back from that encounter with a limp.

Divine faithfulness [is] shown to us in God's increasing desire for intimacy. At first God was the God for us, our protector and shield. Then, when Jesus came, God became the God with us, our companion and friend. Finally, when Jesus sent His Spirit, God was revealed to us as the God within us, our very breath and heartbeat.

Henri Nouwen

Can you see a progression in your understanding of God? In your relationship with Him? Write about it or illustrate it.

Sometimes our early impressions of God need to be modified. "Gentle Jesus, meek and mild" may need to get some guts, or the great judge who sits upon His throne may need to be tempered with mercy within our minds. Write about what you may have learned as a child that needs to be corrected.

_____

_____

_____

_____

_____

_____

_____

THE INTROSPECTIVE CORNER

Who is God to me today?

> The reason I can still find hope
> is that I keep this one thing in mind:
> the Lord's mercy.
> We were not completely wiped out.
> His compassion is never limited.
> It is new every morning.
> His faithfulness is great.
>
> *Lamentations 3:21-23, God's Word*

> Jesus bore little resemblance to (my previous images). For one thing, he was far less tame. Other people affected Jesus deeply—obstinacy frustrated him, self-righteousness infuriated him, simple faith thrilled him. He seemed more emotional and spontaneous than the average person, not less.
>
> *Philip Yancey*

God is described in various ways throughout the Scriptures. **Attributes** are characteristics of God, such as holiness, mercy, justice, all-powerful, everywhere present, all-knowing, etc. List three attributes of God that you most connect with at this time in your life, and note why they speak to you.

Example: mercy, because I have messed up so many times and He still forgives me

Attribute: _____

_____

_____

Attribute: _____

_____

_____

Attribute: _____

_____

_____

Images are pictures that can be used as metaphors for God, such as *shepherd, bread, door*. Think of an image of God from the scriptures that you can visualize, and indicate why you chose it, what God looks like, and what you look like.

Example: shepherd—because I really need someone to take care of me—He looks like a scrubby old guy with a stick—I look well cared-for

Image: _____

_____

_____

_____

_____

Stories are a third way that God reveals Himself to His people, such as the prodigal son who returns to the embrace of the waiting father. Name one biblical story that describes God to you and why you think you identify with that story. Spend some time visualizing yourself in that story.

Example: Samson—because I try to make it in my own strength

Story: _____

_____

_____

_____

_____

_____

_____

> Those who believe they believe in God,
> but without passion in the heart,
> without anguish of mind, without uncertainty,
> without doubt, and even at times without despair,
> believe only in the idea of God, and not in God himself.
> *Madeleine L'Engle*

John Wesley told of a strange warming that came over him during an encounter with God. How in your body do you experience God and how do you physically express passion for God?

Example: lifting hands, chills, a trance-like state, tears

_____

_____

_____

_____

_____

_____

> One with an anesthetized heart
> hears God with Israel's ears.
> *Brent Curtis and John Eldredge*

Just as we can welcome the presence of God in a physical way, we are also able to turn off our bodies and minds to the presence of God. In what way have you allowed your heart or mind to be anesthetized (hardened, numb)?

_____

_____

_____

_____

_____

Do you have an anesthetic of choice?

fantasy

drugs   **pride**

arrogance

alcohol

pornography

indifference

food

television

workaholism   **despair**

Fill in the blank _____

There's an ache inside if you get quiet enough.
Liz Shella

When was the last time you were completely quiet for five minutes … for an hour … for a day? Describe that experience.

_____

_____

_____

_____

_____

I was teaching a Sunday School class of second and third graders when one of the children said, "You can't really hear God talking." Before I got a chance to give the child my biblically based, theologically correct, age-appropriate response, 7-year-old Angel chimed in with what needed to be said: "You can if you get quiet enough!"

There is a large, leisurely center to existence
where God must be deeply pondered, lovingly believed.
Eugene Peterson

The center where I encounter God in my life looks like:

AN EMERGING VISION

How will I experience God in my tomorrows?

Imagine yourself walking into an art gallery made up of a number of small
rooms. The first contains portraits of God that you recognize from the early
years of your life. The second room is lined with pictures that reflect God's
presence and person in your life today. Beyond these two rooms stretch a
number of God Galleries, rooms that beckon you to enter.

Abba

Breath

Bridegroom

Chief Musician

Creator

Father

Lily of the Valley

Morning Star

Mother

Fire

Potter

Lamb

Rock

Shield

Warrior

Shepherd

Nurturer

For me, this expedition into the gallery of God was life-changing. I had not thought much about who God was beyond my early sense of Him, so moving into the various chambers and realizing that there were so many more rooms and portraits than I could have imagined blew me away. Because I'm a verbal person, I explored these galleries through poetry—that of others and then, ultimately, my own. Trying to find the right words and images to communicate who God was becoming to me was a wonderfully freeing experience. I'd encourage you to find a way to share your broadening view of God with others.

I continue to want a cozy, loving God who helps me to escape the difficult stages of transformation, rather than a God who leaves me empty and who refuses to rescue me from my darkness until I've learned from it.

Joyce Rupp

desert

provision
hunger's ache
angel-bread manna, bitter-sweet water
broom-tree sustenance, baptizer's locust, honey
heart's cry
stripped-naked longings, renewed passions
wasteland redeemed

presence
mystical manifestation
burning bush, fiery pillar
biting wind, scorching sun
veiled deity
silence
bedrock conviction
wilderness restored

jas

To seek God and only God, not thoughts about God or answers to life's questions, is demanding, and at the same time supremely generous and self-transcendent.

Barbara Metz and John Burchill

As you ponder new images of God, what are one or two aspects of His personality, His being, that you are being drawn to?

_____

_____

_____

_____

_____

What are the images of God from the Scriptures that you avoid?

_____

_____

_____

_____

_____

Consider how you might work to integrate the difficult images into your understanding of God.

_____

_____

_____

_____

_____

The closer I get to God,
the denser the mists
until the fog of mystery becomes smoky-rich.

Leonard Sweet

When you encounter the "fog of mystery," what do you do with it?
Circle one or more.

run away   **try to figure it out**

ignore it

rest in it

turn on the lights

embrace it

rationalize it

talk about it

deny it

Write about your experience of the mystery.

_____

_____

_____

_____

_____

_____

You will seem to know nothing and to feel nothing except a
naked intent toward God in the depths of your being. Try as
you might, this darkness and this cloud will remain between you
and your God ... but learn to be at home in this darkness.
Return to it often, letting your spirit cry out to him whom you
love. He whom man cannot grasp by knowledge can be
embraced by love.

The Cloud of Unknowing

In C.S. Lewis's *The Lion, the Witch and the Wardrobe*, the children ask the beavers about Aslan (the Christ figure). "Aslan is a Lion—the Lion, the great Lion" is the response. "Is he quite safe?" "Course he isn't safe. But he's good. He's the King, I tell you."

Seeking to know God more deeply is not safe, if safe is defined as being protected from disruption. But God is good, and He desires to move us closer to Him, and to use us in ways we can hardly comprehend.

Use this space to write or draw an image of God you would like to explore further, even though it may not feel safe.

Make ready for the Christ, whose smile—like lightning—sets free the song of everlasting glory that now sleeps in your paper flesh like dynamite.

Thomas Merton

TO JOIN THE DANCE

It is said that there is a certain road that is paved with good intentions. Commit now to taking a next step on another road, the road toward knowing God.

First steps ...

- Set aside time to explore a new image of God, for a half day, weekend, or one hour each week.
- Keep a written record of the God images you see over the next four weeks.
- Create an icon (not an idol) that represents God.
- Write a story about yourself and God.
- Address God in prayer using different names, images.
- Use guided meditation to see God in a new way.
- Write a psalm of yearning for God (see Psalm 42 for an example).
- Sing your prayer of longing. Start with Steve Green's "Oh, I Want to Know You More," or Babbie Mason's "To the Cross," and then your own.
- Read an account of Jesus' interaction with someone in the Gospel, and put yourself in the story. Become Peter, the woman at the well, Mary, Thomas, Lazarus. Think about what God looks like, what Jesus looks like from that vantage point.
- Consider whether there is a predominant metaphor your faith tradition uses for God, or uses to describe itself, and ponder that.

As a commitment to join the dance, today I will seek to know God more deeply by:

_____

_____

_____

_____

_____

For the future, the step I will take in seeking after God will be:

_____

_____

_____

_____

_____

_____

_____

_____

_____

You will seek me and find me
when you seek me with all your heart.

Jeremiah 29:13, NIV

at His feet

prostrate
exposed carnality
nakedness revealed, depravity reviled
stone-barren heart crushed, crucified
conviction

seated
absorbed in presence
distractions silenced, demons handcuffed
word incarnate in soul-penetration
awe

kneeling
rite of homage
impassioned devotion, reverent worship
saint-hands clasped in petition, raised in exaltation
adoration

jas

Prayer ...

Who are You, God? As I wrestle with that question, keep me from demanding an answer so that I can attempt to control You in my life. Enable me to rest in the knowledge that the "I am," the God of the people of Israel, is also the God of the twenty-first century. But continue to draw me to Yourself, with the desire to see You more clearly, love You more dearly, and follow You more nearly, day by day. In the name of the One who was, and is, and is to come,

Amen.

> For now we see through a glass, darkly; but then face to face.
> *I Corinthians 13:12, KJV*

Heartwork ...

(space to think, write, pray, feel)

_____

_____

_____

_____

_____

_____

_____

_____

_____

_____

_____

_____

_____

BREAD FOR THE SOUL

Scripture

Jeremiah 9

Philippians 2

Colossians 1

Film

Simon Burch

Les Miserables (or see it on stage if you can)

Music

"Hymn," Paul Stookey

"Come Home," Wayne Watson

"Oh, I Want to Know You More," Steve Green

"Shepherd of My Heart," Mark Baldwin and Dick Tunney

"All I Once Held Dear" ("Knowing You"), Graham Kendrick

"To the Cross," Babbie Mason

"Breath of Heaven," Amy Grant

The Written Word

God in the Dark, Luci Shaw

The Jesus I Never Knew, Philip Yancey

The Idea of the Holy, Rudolph Otto

Reaching for the Invisible God, Philip Yancey

Ragman and Other Cries of Faith, Walter Wangerin

Finding God, Larry Crabb

The Sacred Romance: Drawing Closer to the Heart of God, Brent Curtis and John Eldredge

Moments with the Saviour series, Ken Gire

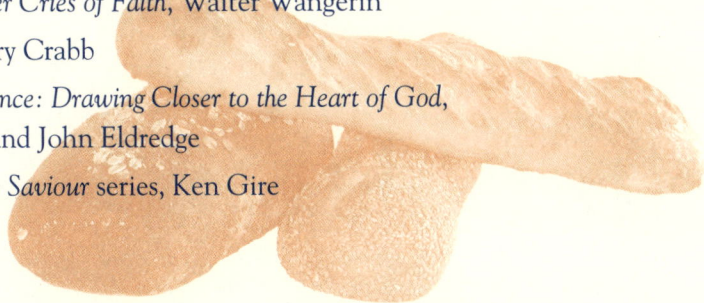

PURPOSE

THE PRELUDE

The author of the book of Ecclesiastes struggles with the question of meaning and purpose. Why am I here? What is life all about? Is it just smoke, nothing but smoke? Or is there purpose to life, is there a purpose for me in life?

I wrestle with the question of purpose. Some wrestling comes from a good place, one which longs to express my faith in meaningful ways that will bring glory to God. But I also struggle with a prideful desire to have impact, to have others notice how gifted I am, how hard I work, how spiritual I can be. Yuck!

One night, God powerfully got my attention. In preparing to send children to camp, I sat treating hair and combing out nits, a tedious and far-from-glorious task.

I did it because having lice would mean these girls couldn't stay at camp, and they needed that experience badly. Of course, the voice in my head screamed, "You went to seminary for this?" But as I silenced that voice, I was able to hear the Spirit of God whisper, "This is what I've called you to for this moment, for these daughters of Mine, to touch with the gentle hands of Christ, to speak words of grace that are without shame. This is where I need you today."

THE REFLECTING POOL

What have I lived for?

> These are the things I go over and over, emptying out the
> pockets of my life.
>
> *Psalm 42:4, The Message*

What were you purposeful about as a child?

Example: I always wanted to befriend the outsider of the group.

_____

_____

_____

_____

_____

_____

_____

_____

_____

_____

> The place God calls you to is the place where your deep
> gladness and the world's hunger meet.
>
> *Frederick Buechner*

Those things we feel passionate about, what we would make sacrifices for, can help to define our purposes in life. Describe what called forth your passion as a teenager.

Example: sports, music, world hunger

_____

_____

_____

_____

_____

_____

In particular for teens, the music they listen to speaks volumes about what matters to them. What music did you listen to when you were a teenager?

Example: "Yellow Submarine," "Imagine," "Stairway to Heaven" (I know, I'm dating myself!)

_____

_____

_____

_____

_____

_____

Look back on your life
and put frames around the things that brought you joy...
[We must] listen to the voice of our own gladness.
                                                    Ken Gire

As Gire suggests, put a frame around one of your experiences that brought you joy, by writing or drawing about it.

What were the factors that led you to choose the field you are currently working in?

_____

_____

_____

_____

_____

If there had been no limits (finances, opportunity, time, etc.) what would you have done with your life?

Example: astronaut, Cleveland Browns football player, pianist

_____

_____

_____

_____

_____

_____

Jot down words or phrases that describe the feelings you have about what might be considered lost opportunity.

THE INTROSPECTIVE CORNER

What do I live for today?

> He has told you, O mortal, what is good;
> and what does the Lord require of you
> but to do justice, and to love kindness,
> and to walk humbly with your God?
>
> *Micah 6:8, NRSV*

> God is in the process of changing what we desire, far more
> than he is in the process of giving us what we desire.
>
> *Charles Stanley*

What, today, in your living (thinking, feeling, doing), has brought you joy?

_____

_____

_____

_____

_____

> Lord, whatever you give me to do,
> I pray neither my self nor the work
> will stand in the way of others seeing your glory.
>
> *Unknown*

What today, in your living (thinking, feeling, doing), has brought God glory?

_____

_____

_____

_____

Ministry means the ongoing attempt to put one's own search for God, with all the moments of pain and joy, despair and hope, at the disposal of those who want to join this search but do not know how.

Henri Nouwen

How would you describe your participation in ministry?

Example: working in a soup kitchen, mentoring a younger person

_____

_____

_____

_____

_____

How has your ministry impacted another individual during the past week?

_____

_____

_____

_____

_____

How is your ministry changing you?

_____

_____

_____

_____

_____

If I can look at my life with a kind of holy penetration and sense that God is telling me "well done," I need to assent to his evaluation, and praise him that he who began a good work in me is continuing it.

Luci Shaw

What is God affirming in your life just now?

_____

_____

_____

_____

_____

I want to be creative like you, Father.
I want to enjoy all kinds of people.
Give me the creative freedom of your spirit.
Silence my censors, and awaken the slumbering artist within.
Give me a new song to sing, a new story to write.

Richard Kriegbaum

How is God's creative freedom being expressed in your life today?

_____

_____

_____

_____

_____

Our illusions of perfection melt like ice shavings on hot asphalt, only to be replaced by the sweet taste of real life in its fragile yet intimate unfolding. We cannot push against the pace of grace.

Susan Muto

Recently, I was without the use of my computer for three days due to an upgrade that had to take place. I went nuts! I was so used to being able to access my e-mail, get on the Internet when I wanted to, and write what needed to be written. Have you tried using a typewriter lately? Do you even have one that works? (And here I am, wanting you to write by hand!) Our culture is consumed by "instant," and so am I in many ways. Microwaves, fast foods, e-mail, cell phones, all speak to immediate gratification, immediate access. We are persons (yes, I admit I am in this too) who have little tolerance for waiting. Yet God does not operate at my beck and call, and I'm realizing more and more that He places a high value on patience, one of the fruits of the Spirit (Galatians 5). When I recently gave our congregation the chance to choose the fruit of the Spirit that they desired, patience was the first to go—oh, I mean, to be chosen. Fancy that!

Eugene Peterson uses the phrase "passionate patience" in a number of the psalms in his paraphrase, *The Message*. Where in your life do you see yourself having "passionate patience"?

_____

_____

_____

_____

> The need to wait for Christ from heaven will rescue us from the presumption which thinks we can do everything. The need to work for Christ on earth will rescue us from the pessimism which thinks we can do nothing. Only a Christian mind which has developed a Biblical perspective can enable us to preserve this balance.
>
> *John Stott*

Where do you place yourself today on this continuum in relationship to your work? In relationship to God?

1   2   3   4   5   6   7   8   9   10

I Can Do Everything ⟷ I Can Do Nothing

There are two basic ways [to serve God]: run errands for God—feed the hungry, love the poor, fight on His side and the like. The other way to serve Him is to do things you need to do because He is God and you are one of His children. Like singing songs for Him, laughing for Him, shedding a tear for Him, telling Him what's on your mind.

William Willimon

Think about your day today. Write down the things you've done or plan to do that fit Willimon's description.

Errands for God	Because you are a child of God

If we have a purpose of our own, it destroys the simplicity and leisureliness which ought to characterize the children of God. Jesus led every one [of his disciples] to the place where their hearts were broken.

Oswald Chambers

Going through the motions
doesn't please you,
a flawless performance is nothing to you.
I learned God-worship
when my pride was shattered.
Heart-shattered lives ready for love
don't for a moment escape God's notice.
Psalm 51:16-17, The Message

Where in a typical day is your heart broken by what you see in your neighborhood, in the media, in your family, in your workplace?

_____

_____

_____

How have you translated that heartbreak into action this week?

_____

_____

_____

Were you able to write anything in the above lines? If not, what would it take to be moved by the things that break the heart of God?

_____

_____

_____

Where you are right now
is God's place for you.
Live and obey
and
love and believe
right there.
I Corinthians 7:17, The Message

AN EMERGING VISION

What do I hope to do?

> … Being confident of this, that he who began a good work in you will carry it on to completion until the day of Christ Jesus.
>
> *Philippians 1:6, NIV*

> Acceptance of the creative will of God, and effectively doing what we perceive to be that will with courage and indifference to personal obstacles, is the secret of real success in the Kingdom.
>
> *Benedict Groeschal*

What does God want you to do with the rest of your life? Whether it is to move to the mission field or to model kindness in your neighborhood, following God takes courage.

What might that courage look like for you? Consider whom it might involve, where it might lead, what it may cost.

_____

_____

_____

_____

_____

> Greed and holiness are both options. To steer away from the former and towards the latter takes courage, self-awareness and grace.
>
> *Ralph Harper*

> … a call is not an event, but an ongoing dynamic of a growing and powerful claim. One's embrace of a sense of call may mature in time and grow beyond the innocence of the outset.
>
> *Walter Brueggemann*

God makes His will known to His people in various ways. How has God led you to make decisions in the past? Check all that apply:

- ☐ burning bush
- ☐ night of prayer
- ☐ counsel of friends and family
- ☐ directed to specific Scripture
- ☐ listing pros and cons
- ☐ flipping a coin
- ☐ day of solitude
- ☐ spiritual direction
- ☐ reading
- ☐ at the shore
- ☐ on a mountaintop
- ☐ fasting

In searching for God's guidance for your future, you may want to revisit ways He has directed you in the past or you may want to undertake a new discipline to seek His heart. How will you seek to look and listen for God's direction this week in a way that you have used before?

_____

_____

_____

_____

How will you seek to look and listen for God's direction this week in a new way?

_____

_____

_____

_____

Anne Lamott tells of her pastor's illustration of getting direction from God in prayer. When she prays for direction, one spot of illumination always appears just beyond her feet, a circle of light into which she can step. In the same way, in our faith work we stumble toward where we think we're supposed to go, bumbling along, and here is what's so amazing—we actually end up finding ourselves exactly where we're supposed to be. Draw a sketch of yourself stepping into the next circle of light, or write about that experience.

Intimate union with God leads to the most creative involvement in the contemporary world.

Henri Nouwen

Use this space to match your dreams (from the first section, Journey), with what you've discovered about your purposes in life.

Dream	+ Purpose	= Vision
to write	minister to women	write a book for women about Wisdom

The thing is to stalk your calling in a certain skilled and supple way, to locate the most tender and live spot and plug into that pulse. This is yielding, not fighting... Yielding at every moment to the perfect freedom of single necessity.

Annie Dillard

What are the obstacles that keep you from following your purpose (what God desires for you)? Choose one purpose in your life and brainstorm what can be done to overcome the obstacles in your path.

My PURPOSE is ...

_____

_____

The OBSTACLE(S) I face are ...

_____

_____

What I can do to OVERCOME obstacle(s) is ...

_____

_____

Lord, let me dream of higher ground,
Challenge my thinking, show me your way,
Let not contentment keep me bound,
Nor fear defeat me, Lord, I pray.

Give me new vision for the lost,
Suffering, broken, hungry, afraid,
I am Your servant at any cost,
Empower my life, begin today.

Then through faith's vision, let me soar,
From earth's allure, to heaven's heights,
Feast at the table, bow and adore,
O lift the veil, I would see Christ.

(to be sung to the tune "Maryton" —
"O Master, Let Me Walk With Thee")

jas

From Jesus I learn that, whatever activism I get involved in, it must not drive out love and humility, or otherwise I betray the kingdom of heaven.

Phillip Yancey

I had the privilege of spending time with a dear friend who had had a serious stroke a number of months before. He is a man of deep convictions, but there had always been a happy-go-lucky air to him. He had been serving in a major administrative position within our denomination prior to the stroke, and at the time of our conversation was serving in a temporary office assignment while he was working through his therapy. As he was not sure if his physical limitations would allow him to assume his previous position, there had been discussion as to where he might be able to be assigned when he completes therapy. He said to me, with tears streaming down his face (and mine), "I hope that we can become pastors to a small church in New York City, because I just want to be able to tell the people about Jesus." That is purpose defined.

If you could only do three things in what remains of your lifetime, what would they be?

1. _____

_____

_____

_____

2. _____

_____

_____

_____

3. _____

_____

_____

_____

I truly want to follow you, but I also want to follow my own desires and lend an ear to the voices that speak about prestige, success, human respect, pleasure, power and influence. Help me to become deaf to these voices and more attentive to your voice, which calls me to choose the narrow road to life.

Henri Nouwen

TO JOIN THE DANCE

First steps ...

- Read slowly through the Gospels, writing explicit directions, one on a page, regarding what God is asking you to do.

- Seek out someone who can be a spiritual guide.

- Write a personal mission statement.

- Give yourself to something you can feel strong passion for.

- Eliminate "I'll try" from your vocabulary for a week.

- At the end of the day, ask yourself the questions; When did I feel most alive today? When did I most feel life draining out of me today?

- Determine to practice "passionate patience" in one area of your life for the next month.

- Be aware of what brings you to tears, what makes your blood boil — and find a way to respond in action.

---

holy discontent

plunged into churning rapids
fueled by restless wonderings, hallowed heart hunger
a sacred burr under saddle, spurring on dreams of redemption
a spirit-wind stirring

jas

Romans 12:9-10 encourages us to ...

- love people genuinely

- hate sin passionately

- hold truth tenaciously

- express mutual affection unashamedly

- honor others openly

As you consider those words, which phrase is easiest for you and why?

_____

_____

_____

Which is hardest and why?

_____

_____

_____

What first step could you take to embrace the hardest phrase?

_____

_____

_____

_____

I came here (Puget Sound) to study hard things—
rock and sea salt—
and to temper my spirit on their edges.
"Teach me your ways, O Lord" is,
like all prayers,
a rash one,
and one I cannot but recommend.

Annie Dillard

In taking the next step to discover, confirm, and follow God's purpose in my life, I will:

_____

_____

_____

_____

_____

Prayer ...

Master Designer, You have burdened my heart with the needs of others, and with a desire for my life to have significance for Your Kingdom. Make my ears receptive to Your voice, make my heart sensitive to the Spirit's nudge, and make my feet willing to walk the path that You direct me to, whether it be wide or narrow, smooth or rocky, crowded or lonely. Might I use the gifts You have given to me in ways that bring glory to You. In the name of Jesus, the One who knew that He must be about his Father's business,

Amen.

Heartwork ...

(space to think, write, pray, feel)

BREAD FOR THE SOUL

Scripture

Acts of the Apostles

Joshua 4

Films

Spitfire Grill

Patch Adams

Music

"Not Too Far From Here," Ty Lacy and Steve Siler

The Written Word

Bold Purpose, Dan Allender and Tremper Longman

Upside Down: The Paradox of Servant Leadership, Stacey Rinehart

What Color is Your Parachute? Richard Nelson Bolles

The Little Prince, Antoine de Saint-Exupéry

The Velveteen Rabbit, Margery Williams

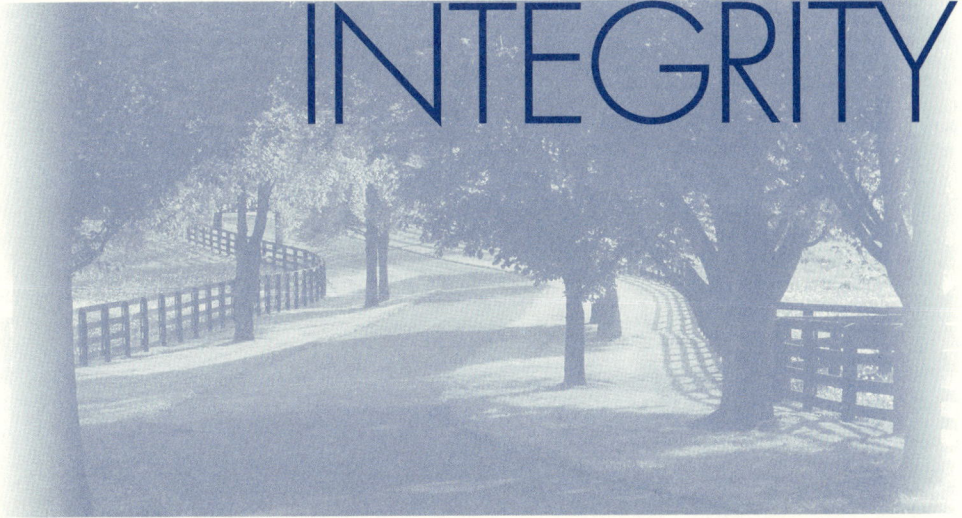

INTEGRITY

THE PRELUDE

Is there a wholeness in me?

> He is a shield for those who walk in integrity
> in order to guard those on paths of justice
> and to watch over the way of his godly ones.
> Then you will understand
> what is right and just and fair —
> every good course in life.
>
> *Proverbs 2:7-9, God's Word*

The concept of integrity in this context is a broad one. God's plan is for us to live integrated lives, in which our words, actions, and emotions are consistent with each other and with what we profess to believe. Integrity involves being fair and honest in relationships and business dealings. It incorporates the desire and demand for justice, especially for those who are powerless. It is more easily described than defined.

THE REFLECTING POOL

Has my life been one of integrity?

> Create in me a pure heart, O God,
> and renew a steadfast spirit within me.
> Do not cast me from your presence
> or take your Holy Spirit from me.
> Restore to me the joy of your salvation
> and grant me a willing spirit, to sustain me.
> *Psalm 51:10-12, NIV*

It has been said that integrity is defined by what we do when no one is looking. Integrity springs from an integration of faith and action, known as praxis.

Think back to your childhood. What was a lesson that you learned about integrity?

Example: your mother telling the cashier that she gave her too much change

_____

_____

_____

_____

_____

What were issues in which you desired justice while you were growing up?

Example: standing up to a bully, the Vietnam War, political corruption

_____

_____

_____

_____

_____

A life of integrity does not just happen. It flows from convictions that are held firm, and which then impact thinking, feeling, and behavior. For example, a conviction that life is precious and God-ordained might lead someone to work to change the abortion law. A conviction that all people should have equal rights to resources might direct someone to work for civil rights or economic redistribution. What are the core convictions about people, the world, and God that have directed your life?

People

_____

_____

_____

_____

_____

The World

_____

_____

_____

_____

God

_____

_____

_____

_____

_____

> Does the motive of a sin—
> its rationale, its reason—
> make it any less a sin?
> Isn't the betrayal of the sovereignty of the Lord in our lives
> always a sin,
> regardless of the factors that drove us to betray Him?
> Yet we habitually defend ourselves
> and diminish our fault by referring to reasons why we "had to"
>   do it.
> Motives console us.
>
> *Walter Wangarin*

A life of integrity is one that is cognizant of its sinful behaviors, thoughts, and emotions. Have you ever prayed, "Lord, show me my sin?" If so, what has He revealed to you?

_____

_____

_____

_____

_____

If you have never prayed that prayer, are you willing to today? What would He say to you?

_____

_____

_____

_____

_____

Recognition must lead to repentance—expressing sorrow, asking for forgiveness, and then moving in a different direction.

Think of a time in your past when that has happened. Write or draw about it.

God, you are absolutely who you claim to be.
Keep me true to myself.

Richard Kriegbaum

THE INTROSPECTIVE CORNER

Am I who I claim to be?

> The integrity of the upright guides them.
>
> *Proverbs 11:3, NIV*

> None of us will escape the moment when we have to decide whether to withdraw, to play it safe, or to act upon what we prayerfully believe to be right... knowing we will probably be punished by those who do not want universe-disturbers to stand up and be counted.
>
> *Madeleine L'Engle*

Make a list of five value statements that you use in guiding your living.

Example: People matter more than rules.

1. _____

_____

2. _____

_____

3. _____

_____

4. _____

_____

5. _____

_____

Martin Luther King Jr. made a distinction in regards to the definition of peace. He believed that negative peace was simply the absence of tension, but that positive peace was the presence of justice. It would seem easier to achieve a negative peace by ignoring what is wrong in the family or culture (being willing to continue to sit in the back of the bus).

Do you desire a positive peace enough to be willing to risk conflict, to stand up for what is right? Name one area in your life where you will move towards desiring justice.

Example: providing safety and support for domestic violence targets

_____

_____

_____

_____

_____

> [I am] only little by little coming to understand that the most precious thing I have to give them is not whatever words I have to say but simply whatever, spoken or unspoken, I have in me of Christ, which is also the most precious thing they have to give me.
>
> *Frederick Buechner*

Asking questions of ourselves can shine light on our motivations and our actions. Think on, write about, or meditate on the following questions:

How do you handle life when you do not get what you want?

_____

_____

_____

_____

_____

In what situations do you hold back from offering yourself to others?

_____

_____

_____

When do you struggle to trust?

_____

_____

_____

> Faithfulness is the inner power of life which enables us to understand ourselves. As you observe other people, you will see how few of them are faithful. And yet, as we look at the few who are, it makes us yearn to become more faithful as they are.
> *Albert Schweitzer*

Integrity also involves doing what is right without demanding to be noticed or rewarded.

> God has not called us to be successful;
> he has called us to be faithful.
> *Mother Teresa*

faithful

vine
hearts rooted in blessed assurance
abiding in presence, clinging to Christ
sustained by water of life, bread of heaven
hope eternal

remnant
fragment enduring in steadfast purpose
obedience embraced, commitment kept
anchored in limitless love, measureless mercy
grace amazing

jas

THE EMERGING VISION

How can I seek integrity and justice?

It's who you are and the way you live that count before God.
Your worship must engage your spirit in the pursuit of truth.
That's the kind of people the Father is out looking for:
those who are simply and honestly *themselves*
before Him in their worship.

John 4:23, The Message

We have become insensitized to evil—
we are only a little sad—
or silly.

Paul Rader

In a typical day what outrages you in what you see in your neighborhood, in the media, or in your workplace?

_____

_____

_____

_____

_____

_____

_____

_____

It says something about our times that we rarely use the word
sinful, except to describe a really good dessert.

William Ferrell

How has that outrage translated into action this week?

_____

_____

_____

_____

_____

If it hasn't, should it? How?

_____

_____

_____

_____

_____

> What is justice?
> To be right, or to appear right?
>
> _Charles Colson_

It was in reading William Bennett's The Death of Outrage _that I recognized that his title perfectly describes what happened in our society through the past decade. For outrage is on its last legs, if not already dead. Reading the report of Jesse Jackson, who admitted to an affair and to fathering a child in that relationship, I saw the same response—no outrage. In fact, Marshall Frady predicted that "this might, as it did with King, lend him a complexity that enhances the moral grandeur of the man." We become more upset over the latest cancellation of a favorite TV show than over our President committing perjury, a prominent minister fathering a child outside of marriage, or how nasty I am to my husband. Where is our outrage? Where is my outrage?_

What injustice makes your blood boil today?

_____

_____

_____

_____

_____

What are you doing about that?

_____

_____

_____

_____

_____

Charles Colson defines integrity as:

- to be what we claim to be
- to do what we claim to do
- to give what we claim to give
- to claim only what we have truly given, done and been for God and the people

Integrity that has been damaged by our actions can be restored through God's grace and our hard work, but the consequences of our choices cannot be changed. Once our character is marked by dishonesty, adultery, or unkindness, we cannot rid ourselves of the scar, but can only accept the redemptive power of God, allowing Him to use our weakness for His glory.

> A failure of nerve and an unwillingness to risk
> distorts God into a bookkeeper
> and the gospel of grace is swapped
> for the security of religious bondage.
>
> _Brennan Manning_

Read Psalm 51. In the spirit of David's plea, write out your prayer of repentance, and your desire for restoration.

In what area of your life is God calling you to take a stand for justice?

What might that stand cost you?

TO JOIN THE DANCE

First steps ...

- Write out your personal definition of integrity.
- Get involved in a cause that you believe in, such as pro-life, AIDS ministry, crisis pregnancy center, anti-pornography campaign, foster parenting, children's advocacy, prison ministry, or a political campaign for candidates who have positions you have convictions about.
- Ask God to show you your sin.
- Write a psalm of repentance.
- Read about abolition, civil rights, the persecution of the church around the world.
- Look through your checkbook over the last six months—does it reflect your values and passions?

In seeking to live a life of integrity, I will:

_____

_____

_____

_____

_____

In seeking to work for justice, I will:

_____

_____

_____

_____

_____

Prayer ...

Holy, Holy, Holy, Lord God Almighty, as I dare to approach Your purity and righteousness, help me to recognize my own sinfulness. Cover my sin with Your grace. Knowing that You are the source of righteousness and the foundation of justice in the world, I ask You to place within my heart a longing for integrity and a passion for justice. In the name of the One who sits at the right hand of the Father,

Amen.

Heartwork ...

(space to think, write, pray, feel)

_____

_____

_____

_____

_____

_____

_____

_____

_____

_____

_____

_____

_____

_____

_____

_____

_____

BREAD FOR THE SOUL

Scripture

Nehemiah

Daniel

Habbakuk

Film

The Mission

Cadence

Music

"Breathe in Me," Michael W. Smith

The Written Word

Leadership Prayers, Richard Kriegbaum

Christianity for Modern Pagans, Peter Kreeft

Leaves from the Notebook of a Tamed Cynic, Rudolph Niehbur

Letters from a Birmingham Jail, Martin Luther King, Jr.

The Death of Outrage, William Bennett

A Long Walk to Freedom, Nelson Mandela

An Easy Burden, Andrew Young

Letters from Prison, Dietrich Bonhoeffer

RELATIONSHIP

THE PRELUDE

Who am I with others?

I was brainstorming one day with two young women who have been "welfare moms," trying to determine what their greatest needs were. As we talked, it became apparent that it wasn't simply poverty, lack of education, poor transportation, or inconsistent child care, those social factors we tend to identify with the cycle of dependence. It was the absence of stable relationships in their lives. When the baby got sick, they had no one to take them to the hospital—or to hold their hand. When their world fell apart, there was no one there to help pick up the pieces. And when they had glad news to share, there were very few people in their lives who wanted to listen. It may be, as John Donne wrote, that no man is an island, but it sure feels that way sometimes …

THE REFLECTING POOL

Who has been a part of my life?

> We can't expect our friends to fill us up or to define who we are. Nor would we use our friends as a way of escaping feelings of boredom, emptiness, or self-doubt. To be comfortable with others, we must first be comfortable inside our own skin. To be truly with others, we must first be with ourselves.
>
> *Brenda Hunter*

Who were significant "life-givers" to you as you grew (parents, grandparents, relatives, teacher, pastor, etc.)? Write a brief description of those who played a positive role in your development.

_____ gave me life in the following ways:

_____

_____

_____

_____ gave me life in the following ways:

_____

_____

_____

_____ gave me life in the following ways:

_____

_____

_____

There were other significant people in our life who might be labeled "life-takers." Write a brief description of those who made a negative impact upon your development.

_____ made a negative impact upon me by:

_____

_____

_____ made a negative impact upon me by:

_____

_____

_____ made a negative impact upon me by:

_____

_____

Writing about this may awaken painful feelings in you. Consider finding a way to express them, by talking with a trusted friend, writing a letter, etc. Give some expression to those feelings in the space below.

Forgiveness is a gift that we can offer regardless of the acceptance of responsibility of the other person, and regardless of their response or lack of response. Is there someone on this list from your past that you need to forgive? Write that person's name here. _____ Will you forgive?

THE INTROSPECTIVE CORNER

Who is a part of my circle of relationships today?

List the people in your life who give or take away energy from you:

Give you energy?	Take away energy?

Is there someone in your life today you need to forgive?

_____

_____

Is there someone in your life today you need to ask to forgive you?

_____

_____

> When you forgive, you do not forget the season of cold
> completely, but neither do you shiver in its memory.
> *Paul Coleman*

In front of what person in your life can you fall apart?

_____

_____

Whom can you ask to pray for you or with you (without that person demanding to know the details)?

_____

_____

Whom can you call at 2 a.m., knowing they won't hang up on you?

_____

_____

Whom could you call to bail you out of jail?

_____

_____

> In the state of friendship there is space and freedom for growth,
> that two solitudes protect and touch and greet each other.
> *Rilke*

My friend's mother had been an alcoholic and found sobriety through attending Alcoholics Anonymous for many years. When her mother began to suffer health problems, her AA friends stepped in to help. One of these AA friends told my friend, "Don't worry—we'll check on your mother every day, and make sure she gets what she needs. When the time comes when she can no longer live alone, we'll let you know, and we'll help you both find a place for her." My friend raised the question to me, Would our church do that for us? Would the Christian community rally around us and actually be the body of Christ? The more telling question is, Would I do that for her, for someone in my church? What is the depth of my relationship with others?

> There is always a band of ironic, mournfully jubilant New Orleans minstrels winding its way through the hearts of those who really love.
>
> Mike Mason

Who in your life might fit Mason's description of mournfully jubilant minstrels?

_____

_____

AN EMERGING VISION

Who will be a part of my future?

> If it is possible,
> as far as it depends on you,
> live at peace with everyone.
>
> Romans 12:18, NIV

Committed love is a paradoxical power,
because it is a power to surrender.
Power?
Yes, because sometimes it takes a lot of strength to surrender.
But everything depends on what you surrender.
Committed love is a power to surrender our right to get what
we desire so that the person we love can get what he or she
needs.

Lewis Smedes

Reflecting on Smedes' words, write about two ways in which you could surrender your right to get what you desire so that a person you love can get what he or she needs. Get specific. Name names, times, situations, places.

1. _____

_____

_____

_____

_____

_____

_____

2. _____

_____

_____

_____

_____

_____

_____

Loving well may require that we do something that makes us uncomfortable, or that may disrupt the life of someone we love. Are there places in your relationships where you have to confront something to love well? What might that look like?

_____

_____

_____

_____

_____

Where, in your relationships, do you need to protect yourself?

_____

_____

_____

_____

_____

Where, in your relationships, do you need to learn to put boundaries around your availability?

_____

_____

_____

_____

_____

Love is a feeling to be learned.
It is tension and fulfillment.
It is deep longing and hostility.
It is gladness and it is pain.
There is not one without the other.
Happiness is only a part of love—
this is what has to be learned.
Suffering belongs to love also.
This is the mystery of love, its beauty and its burden.
Love is a feeling to be learned.

Walter Trobisch

Where, in your relationships, do you need to get out of the way so that God can work?

_____

_____

_____

_____

_____

Where, in your relationships, do you need to "go for broke"?

_____

_____

_____

_____

_____

Do not hesitate to love and love deeply. As you love deeply the ground of your heart will be broken more and more, but you will rejoice in the abundance of the fruit it will bear.

Henri Nouwen

What fruit is being birthed in your life? (Galatians 5:22-23) Paint a word picture or make a sketch of that fruit.

The trick is to find a real community, not an insider's club. Not a group that makes believe it is a community, just because everyone recites the same creed. But a community where people care enough to give each other permission to be strugglers, wounded strugglers, who are hanging on to their commitments by their fingernails. A community that cares enough to permit people to fail helps people dare to reveal their own struggles, including their failures as well as successes.

Lewis Smedes

We had spent five years ministering in a large center within an inner city and had struggled to maintain emotional and spiritual equilibrium. When I finally got enough distance from that situation, I was able to recognize that, while we had poured our-selves into the work (and there was always plenty of that), I had not been a part of community. Other than my family, there was no one in my life with whom I prayed, studied the Bible, talked, shared a meal, or cried in front of on any regular basis. Was there anyone in my life who truly knew me? In the midst of a bustling city and a large ministry organization, I felt abandoned. I committed to myself and to God that I would not live that way any longer, that I would find a way to be a part of a "fingernail" community, even if I had to find it person by person, bit by bit. And God has been faithful.

Describe the community (people who love God together) that you are a part of. It may be an organized church, a Bible study group, a friend you meet for coffee once a month.

_____

_____

_____

_____

If it was difficult to name those who are in community with you, consid-er what you might do to become more intentional about developing that "fingernail" community in your life.

_____

_____

_____

_____

_____

TO JOIN THE DANCE

We need quite simply to find places of sharing where the Word can be shared, and where hearts and bread can be broken and passed around.

Richard Rohr

First steps ...

- Cherish your family, and be sure to tell them they are cherished.
- Spend time with someone at least twenty years older than you are, establishing a relationship.
- Find a mentor.
- Become a mentor.
- Seek out a child in your church or neighborhood who needs to be encouraged.
- Invite a friend to move to a deeper level of relationship.
- Bake some cookies, bread, etc., and visit a neighbor with the gift.
- Read through the Gospel of John, asking the question, "How did Jesus love in this situation?" Stop each time you find an answer and write it down.
- At the end of each day, ask yourself the questions: "When did I give and receive the most love today?" "When did I give and receive the least love today?"
- Open your home to others.
- Invite other believers into community by meeting together for prayer, scripture, and hope-sharing.

In my commitment to love well in relationship, I will

_____

_____

_____

In order to invite a deeper relationship, I will intentionally seek out these
people:

_____

_____

_____

Prayer ...

Abba, Father, You are a God who desires relationship with Your children, and
who desires relationships among Your children. Place within me a passion to
know You, not theologically or academically, but intimately. May I be challenged by the words of Jesus to love my brothers and sisters, and to invest my
life in their lives. Challenge me to set aside my fears and my self-protective
strategies, and empower me to move closer to one of Your children today.
Lead me to someone this week who needs the presence of Christ, and give
me the courage to offer that presence. Give me a hunger for community, a
community in which I can be open and vulnerable—and loving. In the name
of the One who first loved me.

Amen.

Love one another as if your lives depended on it.
I Peter 1:22, The Message

Heartwork ...

(space to think, write, pray, feel)

_____

_____

_____

_____

_____

_____

_____

_____

_____

_____

_____

_____

_____

_____

_____

_____

_____

_____

_____

_____

_____

_____

BREAD FOR THE SOUL

Scripture

Ruth

Hosea

Music

"Standing in the Gap," Babbie Mason

The Written Word

Heart to Heart About Men: Words of Encouragement for Women of Integrity, Nancy Groom

Caring and Commitment, Lewis Smedes

Love You Forever, Robert Munsch

Intimate Allies, Dan Allender and Tremper Longman

The Wisdom of Each Other: A Conversation Between Spiritual Friends, Eugene Peterson

Boundaries, Henry Cloud and John Townsend

Exclusion and Embrace, Miraslov Volf

HOPE

THE PRELUDE

May God, the source of hope, fill you with joy and peace
through your faith in him. Then you will overflow with hope by
the power of the Holy Spirit.

Romans 15:13, God's Word

---

*What do people do who have no hope? I found myself asking that question recently
when spending time with a family in the midst of catastrophic illness. As Christians, we
have the hope that God is able to heal. We trust him to be our comfort. And we have
the ultimate hope of heaven, which gives even the most tragic funeral the promise of
joy. It was just a few years ago that we buried a very dear friend, a young man of 19.
We sent him off (his home-going) with strains of "Steppin' on the Clouds" and "When
We All Get to Heaven." I will never forget the depth of emotion at that funeral—the
desperate sorrow that was intermingled with a glorious hope. As the old Gospel song
so clearly reminds us, "I'm possessed of a hope that is steadfast and sure!"*

THE REFLECTING POOL

Have I lived hopefully?

> You know how it feels if you begin hoping for something that you want desperately badly—you almost fight against the hope because it is too good to be true, you've been disappointed so often before.
>
> *C.S. Lewis*

Write about a time in your childhood when your hope was disappointed.

Example: finding out that your parents were Santa Claus

_____

_____

_____

_____

_____

_____

_____

Write about a time in your childhood when your hope was fulfilled.

Example: getting the nicest third-grade teacher

_____

_____

_____

_____

_____

_____

_____

The teen years can be a time of extremes—within a 15-minute period, teens may encounter high hopes and overwhelming frustration and despair. Write about your experience of these extremes.

_____

_____

_____

_____

_____

Life wounds me in the places only hope can reach.
Pat Conroy

Write about a way in which hope has helped to heal a wound in you.

_____

_____

_____

_____

_____

Hope seemed to be in short supply in inner-city Philadelphia. I usually took the in-terstate (supposedly fast) or Kelly Drive (scenic) to our place of ministry in center city, but a couple of times a month I would travel down Ridge Avenue, through the most impoverished neighborhoods of north Philadelphia. I did that to keep myself sensitive to the needs of my people, as well as to the realities of life at its most diffi-cult. However, as I traveled that road, I began to deliberately look for signs of hope. The tulips pushing their way through the soil, the children in their parochial-school uniforms, the well-tended home in the midst of the dilapidated row houses—hope was there, even in the midst of despair. Yet the ultimate hope was symbolized for me in the massive cemetery I would pass on that road—the message that we are waiting "for the blessed hope—the glorious appearing of our great God and Savior, Jesus Christ!"

It would be easy to fall into despair, save one thing—
sometimes as we strain for the rhythm of the spirit,
as we limp when we mean to leap, a miracle takes place.

There, in our apparent, awkward failure, we discover the
meaning of faith, and the reach of grace. When we least
expect it, God takes our frailty, our brokenness, our far-sighted
dreaming and near-sighted execution, and actually uses it to
reveal—in a glimpse—the reality of his kingdom. In our
foolish faithfulness, God becomes present, and offers mercy
and justice and grace and reconciliation in and through our
lives. Even as the saints stumble, people come to Christ, hope is
offered, truth is known, and life finds its way to the dying.
Because of us, and in spite of us.

Dwight Ozark

The loss of hope is a terrible thing to face. Describe a time when you were
without hope.

_____

_____

_____

_____

_____

What helped you turn the corner?

_____

_____

_____

_____

_____

THE INTROSPECTIVE CORNER

Am I facing today's challenges with hope?

Hope accepts mystery
and offers the gift of a solid trust in the unknown.
Hope doesn't pretend that I'll get all I want
nor does hope deny that there will be struggles down the road.
Hope tucks promises of growth and truth
inside the pockets of my struggles.

Joyce Rupp

Look for promises that are tucked in the pockets of the struggles you are having in the present.

Struggle	Growth Promise	Truth Promise
hard time with teen	continuing to love her with strength is possible	God loves her more than I do

Bedrock faith allows me to believe that,
despite the chaos of the present moment,
God does reign;
that regardless of how worthless I may feel,
I truly matter to a God of love;
that no pain lasts forever and no evil triumphs in the end.
Faith sees even the darkest deed of all history,
the death of God's Son,
as a necessary prelude to the brightest.

Phillip Yancey

Fit your experiences into Yancey's categories, and then add the promises God has given you to those listed

Right now in my life	God's Promise
chaos	God reigns—Psalm 46, 11
my worthless feelings	I am loved—Jeremiah 31:3
pain	pain will end—Revelation 21:4
evil	God will triumph—I Corinthians 15:58 "This Is My Father's World"—v.3

Hope is the thing with feathers
that perches in the soul,
and sings the tunes without words and never stops at all.
Emily Dickinson

What tune of hope is singing in your soul today? Write out the melody or sing it to someone today.

This is our hope.
This is the faith with which I return to the South.
With this faith we will be able to hew out of the mountain of despair
a stone of hope.
With this faith we will be able to transform the jangling discords of our nation into a beautiful symphony of brotherhood.
With this faith we will be able to work together,
to pray together, to struggle together, to go to jail together,
to stand up for freedom together,
knowing that we will be free one day.

Martin Luther King, Jr.

Where in your life is hope expressed as passionately as King described his hope in his famous "I Have a Dream" speech?

_____

_____

_____

Where is your dream, rooted in purpose and fueled by hope, taking you?

_____

_____

_____

Hope deferred makes the heart sick,
but a longing fulfilled is a tree of life.

Proverbs 13:12, NIV

AN EMERGING VISION

Will I dare to hope for the future?

The lines of purpose in your lives
never grow slack,
tightly tied as they are
to your future in heaven,
kept taut by hope.

Colossians 1:5, The Message

I have recognized the presence of hope in myself as I have
grown less fearful of myself and others, as I've felt a greater
openness to risk the unknown and the untried, as I've sensed
more of a balance in being and doing and given myself
wholeheartedly in relationships. Images have helped me to
do the patient waiting that is necessary in order for healing
to come.

Joyce Rupp

I found myself in a difficult situation with another person, and I wanted to do what I could to resolve it. A friend asked, "What if nothing changes? What will you do?" At first this was a horrible thought, because not only might the situation not change, but it also had the potential to get worse. While that path of thinking could have easily led me to despair, I realized that I had the ability to choose hope, because even though I had no control over the other person or the circumstances, I did have the ability and desire to change myself, to reject bitterness, to extend mercy, and to move forward in a hopeful pattern of offering grace, and that was the path I needed to take.

How much will you allow yourself to hope?

_____

_____

_____

What are the fears that are keeping you from hoping more?
Example: fear of rejection, fear of disappointment

_____

_____

_____

Choose one area in which you are battling fear. Write out the worst possible scenario that could happen.

_____

_____

_____

Now write out the best possible scenario that could happen.

_____

_____

_____

What will it take to slay the "worst-case scenario" dragons? Write about it, or draw a picture of the dead dragon.

What will it take to give wings to the "best-case scenario" eagles? Write about it, or draw a picture of the soaring eagle (with your name on its wings).

TO JOIN THE DANCE

Hope is a revolutionary patience —
hope begins in the dark,
the stubborn hope that if you just show up and try to do the
    right thing,
the dawn will come.
You wait and watch and work.
You don't give up.

Anne Lamott

First steps ...

- Memorize a hope Scripture verse.

- Pull out a promise of hope each day from the pockets of your struggles.

- Create an image of hope: song, collage, dance, art, quilt, carving.

- Make a list of the reasons for having hope—cut up the list and share with others that need hope.

- Begin your day by singing "Great Is Thy Faithfulness".

- Deliberately search each day for signs of hope, such as a tulip budding, the ocean's rhythmic waves, the blaze of autumn leaves, the eyes of a child.

Hope is not the conviction that something will turn out well,
but the certainty that something makes sense
regardless of how it turns out.
It is hope, above all, which gives us the strength to live
and continually try new things.

Vaclav Havel

In order to face each new day with hope, I will:

_____

_____

_____

_____

Prayer ...

O God of hope, overwhelm me with a sense of hope today. Enable me to look around my life through a hope-filled prism, that fills my sight with your light. Might you "melt the clouds of sin and sadness, and drive the clouds of doubt away." Point me to the cross of Christ, for I pray in the name of the hope-bearer, Jesus.

Amen.

Heartwork ...

(space to think, write, pray, feel)

_____

_____

_____

_____

_____

_____

_____

_____

_____

_____

_____

_____

_____

_____

_____

_____

BREAD FOR THE SOUL

Scripture

Matthew 9:18-26

Luke 15

Film

Spitfire Grill

The Postman

Music

"Great Is Thy Faithfulness," Thomas Chisholm

"In Christ Alone," Shawn Craig and Don Koch

"On Eagle's Wings," Michael Joncas

"He is Able," Rory Noland and Greg Ferguson

"God Will Make a Way," Don Moen

The Written Word

Grey Is the Color of Hope, Irina Ratushinskaya

I Know Why the Caged Bird Sings, Maya Angelou

Disappointment with God, Phillip Yancey

Alexander and the Terrible, Horrible, No Good, Very Bad Day, Judith Viorst

The Return of the Prodigal, Henry Nouwen

IN BENEDICTION

And now, may the God of hope be present to you as you journey for this day. May you be at ease in your own skin, able to accept your gifts and your limitations, your strength and your weakness. May your ever-present desire be to know Christ, and the power of His resurrection, and the fellowship of His suffering. May you be open to the purposes God has planned for you. May you live an integrated life, one marked by personal honor and a yearning for justice. May you love much, and love well. And may you live with a sense of overwhelming hope that impacts the whole of your living, both now and into eternity.

In the name of Jesus,

Amen.

ABOUT THE AUTHOR

JoAnn Streeter Shade has been a Salvation Army officer since 1978. She received a B.A. in sociology from S.U.N.Y. at Binghamton and an M.A. in pastoral counseling from Ashland Theological Seminary. She is currently in the "Women in Prophetic Leadership" doctoral track at Ashland Seminary. Married to Larry, JoAnn is the mother of three sons. She serves as the Salvation Army's divisional social services secretary in Cleveland, Ohio, where she also enjoys participating in the creative arts, including writing, composing music, and playing the piano.